READ
ME
POETRY

A Saucepan On His Head
And Other Nonsense Poems

Acknowledgements

Every effort has been made to obtain permission to reproduce copyright material but there may be cases where we have been unable to trace a copyright holder. The publisher apologizes for any such error and will be happy to correct any omission in future printings.

"I Want to Be Monday" by Charles Causley from ALL DAY SATURDAY published by Macmillan. Reprinted by permission of David Higham Associates

"Nathaniel" by Richard Edwards from TEACHING THE PARROT. Reprinted by permission of the publisher, Faber & Faber Ltd

"I Had a Sausage" and "My Mother Said" from HERE COMES MOTHER GOOSE edited by Iona Opie, illustrated by Rosemary Wells. Published 1999 by Walker Books Ltd, London

"Alas, Alack!" © Walter de la Mare. Reprinted by permission of the Literary Trustees of Walter de la Mare, and the Society of Authors as their Representative

"Dilly Dilly Piccalilli" text © 1971 Clyde Watson, originally illustrated by Wendy Watson. Used by permission of HarperCollins Publishers

"A Saucepan on his Head" from I SAW ESAU edited by Iona and Peter Opie, illustrated by Maurice Sendak. Published 1992 by Walker Books Ltd, London

"There Once Was a Man" by Charles Causley from SELECTED POEMS FOR CHILDREN published by Macmillan. Reprinted by permission of David Higham Associates

"Little Bella" from LULLABIES, LYRICS AND GALLOW SONGS OF CHRISTIAN MORGENSTERN, selected and illustrated by Lisbeth Zwerger. © 1992 Michael Neugebauer Verlag, Verlagsgruppe Nord-Süd Verlag AG, Zürich/Switzerland

"I'd Like to Squeeze" from GET BACK PIMPLE, published by Viking (1996). By kind permission of John Agard c/o Caroline Sheldon Literary Agency

"Lift-off" from COWS MOO, CARS TOOT! by June Crebbin. © 1995 June Crebbin, published by Viking

"Upside Down" from UP THE WINDY HILL by Aileen Fisher. © 1953, © renewed 1981 Aileen Fisher. Used by permission of Marian Reiner for the author

For Andy
P. D.

First published 2001 by Walker Books Ltd
87 Vauxhall Walk, London SE11 5HJ

This edition produced 2002 for
The Book People Ltd, Hall Wood Avenue,
Haydock, St Helens WA11 9UL

2 4 6 8 10 9 7 5 3 1

This selection © 2001 CLPE/LB Southwark
Individual poems © as noted in acknowledgements
Illustrations © 2001 Polly Dunbar

This book has been typeset in Adobe Caslon

Printed in Hong Kong

British Library Cataloguing in Publication Data:
a catalogue record for this book is
available from the British Library

ISBN 0-7445-6883-8

A Saucepan On His Head

And Other Nonsense Poems

Selected by Myra Barrs and Sue Ellis

Illustrated by Polly Dunbar

TED SMART

WHEN I WENT OUT FOR A WALK ONE DAY

When I went out for a walk one day,

My head fell off and rolled away,

And when I saw that it was gone –

I picked it up and put it on.

When I went into the street

Someone shouted, "Look at your feet!"

I looked at them and sadly said,

"I've left them both asleep in bed!"

Anonymous

I Went to the Pictures Tomorrow

I went to the pictures tomorrow

I took a front seat at the back,

I fell from the pit to the gallery

And broke a front bone in my back.

A lady she gave me some chocolate,

I ate it and gave it her back.

I phoned for a taxi and walked it,

And that's why I never came back.

Anonymous

I Want to Be Monday

"I want to be Monday," said Friday.

"It's such a dull spot that I've got.

I'd much rather have it than my day

That comes almost last of the lot."

"What nonsense!" said Tuesday to Thursday.

"I don't think she knows what she's at.

There's no telling which is the worst day

Or which is the best, come to that."

And Wednesday whispered to Sunday,

"I hope Monday doesn't say yes.

I've a feeling by changing the one day

We'll get in a terrible mess."

Said Monday to Friday, "A poor day?
But there's no one of whom we could speak
Who don't thank the stars that it's your day
At the end of a workaday week."

"Of all the seven days," declared Friday,
"I never thought I was the star!
If it's really that happy and high a day
I think I'll leave things as they are.
Yes, I think I'll leave things as they are."

Charles Causley

NATHANIEL

Nathaniel woke up yawning,

"I'm half asleep," he said,

So his left half went down to breakfast

And his right half stayed in bed.

Richard Edwards

GIANT'S WIFE

The terrible giant had a wife

Who was almost twelve feet tall.

She slept with her head in the kitchen

And her feet way out in the hall.

Anonymous

I HAD A SAUSAGE

I had a sausage,
a bonny
bonny sausage,
I put it
in the oven
for my tea.

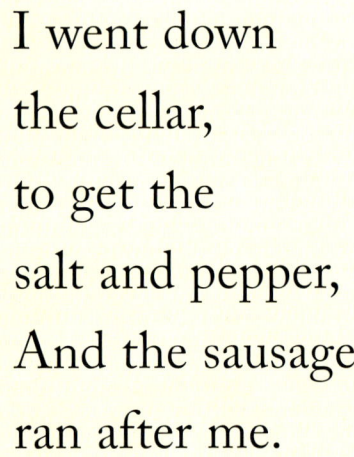

I went down
the cellar,
to get the
salt and pepper,
And the sausage
ran after me.

Anonymous

ALAS, ALACK!

Ann, Ann!
    Come! quick as you can!
There's a fish that *talks*
    In the frying-pan.
Out of the fat,
    As clear as glass,
He put up his mouth
    And moaned "Alas!"
Oh, most mournful,
    "Alas, alack!"
Then turned to his sizzling,
    And sank him back.

Walter de la Mare

DILLY DILLY PICCALILLI

Dilly Dilly Piccalilli

Tell me something very silly:

There was a chap his name was Bert

He ate the buttons off his shirt.

Clyde Watson

A Saucepan on his Head

There was a man who always wore
A saucepan on his head.
I asked him what he did it for –
"I don't know why," he said.
"It always makes my ears so sore,
I am a foolish man.
I think I'll have to take it off,
And wear a frying pan."

Anonymous

There Once Was a Man

There once was a man
Called Knocketty Ned
Who wore his cat
On top of his head.
Upstairs, downstairs,
The whole world knew
Wherever he went
The cat went too.

He wore it at work,
He wore it at play,
He wore it to town
On market-day,
And for fear it should rain
Or the snowflakes fly
He carried a brolly
To keep it dry.

He never did fret
Nor fume because
He always knew
Just where it was.
"And when," said Ned,
"In my bed I lie
There's no better nightcap
Money can buy."

"There's no better bonnet
To be found,"
Said Knocketty Ned,
"The world around.
And furthermore
Was there ever a hat
As scared a mouse
Or scared a rat?"

Did ever you hear
Of a tale like that
As Knocketty Ned's
And the tale of his cat?

Charles Causley

LITTLE BELLA

Here is pretty little Bella
Opening her green umbrella.

    Opening her green umbrella,
    Because it looks like rain, I tell her.

Because it looks like rain, I tell her,
Off you run now, little Bella!

    Off you run now, little one,
    Off to buy a piece of sun.

To buy a piece of sun, you say:
Hello, good day! Hello, good day!

    Hello, good day there, Mr Bunn!
    I want to buy a piece of sun.

I want to buy a piece of sun,
And then the rain will all be done.

    And then the rain will all be done.
    So back inside goes Mr Bunn.

And he will give you, for your money,
A piece of sun like yellow honey.

A piece of sun like yellow honey,
Golden honey, sweet and runny,

Like golden honey from the bee,
And he will pack it up for free.

And he will pack it up for free,
So you can bring it home to me.

And when you're home we'll take it out.
Look, a piece of sun, we'll shout!

Half the sun's for little Bella
Half is for the green umbrella.

So off you go now, little one,
Off to buy a piece of sun.

Christian Morgenstern

MY MOTHER SAID

My mother said
That I never should
Play with the pixies
In the wood;
The wood was dark,
The grass was green,
Up comes Sally
With a tambourine;
I went to the river,
I couldn't get across,
I paid ten shillings
For an old blind horse;
I jumped on his back
And off in a crack,
Sally tell my mother
That I'm coming right back.

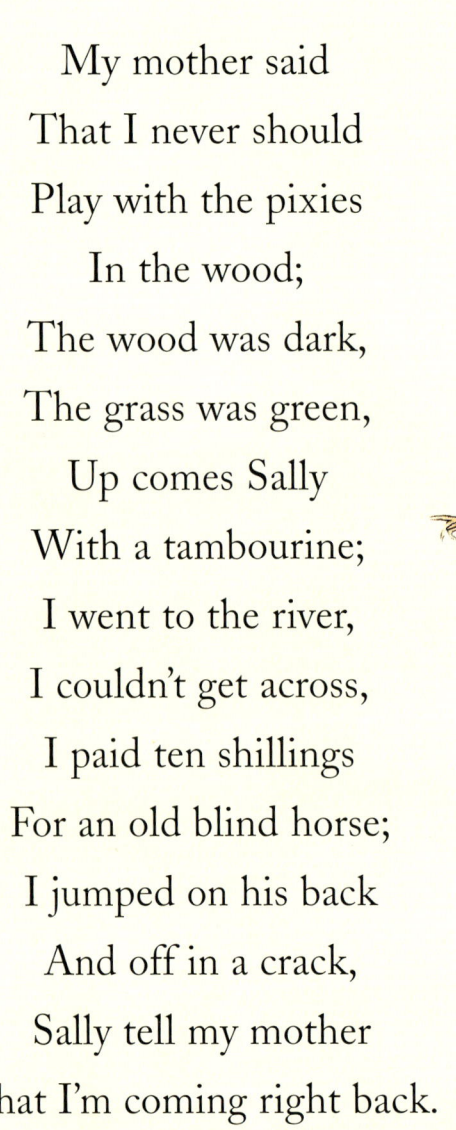

Traditional

THERE WAS AN OLD WOMAN

There was an old woman tossed up in a basket,
Seventeen times as high as the moon;
And where she was going, I couldn't but ask it,
For in her hand she carried a broom.

Old woman, old woman, old woman, quoth I,
O whither, O whither, O whither so high?

To sweep the cobwebs off the sky!

Can I go with you?

Aye, by and by.

Traditional

I Had a Little Brother

I had a little brother
His name was Tiny Tim
I put him in the bathtub
To teach him how to swim

He drank up all the water
He ate up all the soap
He died last night
With a bubble in his throat

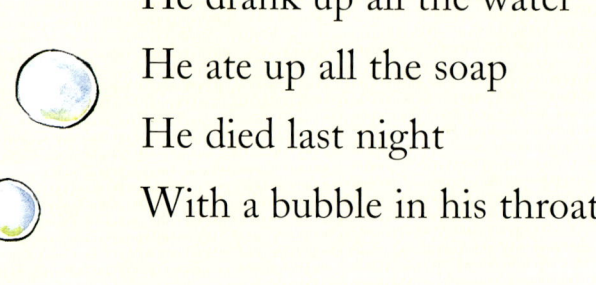

In came the doctor
In came the nurse
In came the lady
With the alligator purse

Dead said the doctor
Dead said the nurse
Dead said the lady
With the alligator purse

Out went the doctor
Out went the nurse
Out went the lady
With the alligator purse.

Traditional

IF ALL THE WORLD WERE PAPER

If all the world were paper,

And all the sea were ink,

If all the trees were bread and cheese,

What should we have to drink?

Anonymous

I'D LIKE TO SQUEEZE

I'd like to squeeze this round world
into a new shape

I'd like to squeeze this round world
like a tube of toothpaste

I'd like to squeeze this world
fair and square

I'd like to squeeze it and squeeze it
till everybody had an equal share

John Agard

LIFT-OFF

Going up,
Going up,
Doors closing,
Doors closing.

Level 2.
Cookshop. Curtains.
Bathrooms and Ladieswear.

Going down,
Going down,
Doors closing,
Doors closing.

Level 1.
Menswear. Childrenswear.
China, Glass and Giftware.

Going up,
Going up,
Doors closing,
Doors closing.

Going down,
Going down,
Doors closing,
Doors –

Wait a minute –
I'm fed up going
Up and down
Down and up.

Boring.
Boring.

Right.
Hang on to your hats!

Going up
Through the roof –

Treetops. Chimney-pots.
Aerials and Birdsong.

Going up,
Going up.

Starlight. Satellites.
Moonbeams and Meteors.

Going up,
Going up...

June Crebbin

UPSIDE DOWN

It's funny how beetles
and creatures like that
can walk upside down
as well as walk flat:

They crawl on a ceiling
and climb on a wall
without any practice
or trouble at all,

While I have been trying
for a year (maybe more)
and still I can't stand
with my head on the floor.

Aileen Fisher

Bed in Summer

In winter I get up at night
And dress by yellow candle-light.
In summer, quite the other way,
I have to go to bed by day.

I have to go to bed and see
The birds still hopping on the tree,
Or hear the grown-up people's feet
Still going past me in the street.

And does it not seem hard to you,
When all the sky is clear and blue,
And I should like so much to play,
To have to go to bed by day?

Robert Louis Stevenson

OTHER READ ME BOOKS

Read Me Beginners are simple rhymes and
stories ideal for children learning to read.

Caveman Dave
Nick Sharratt

Monday Run-day
Nick Sharratt

Mrs Pirate
Nick Sharratt

Pointy-hatted Princesses
Nick Sharratt

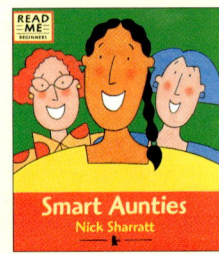
Smart Aunties
Nick Sharratt

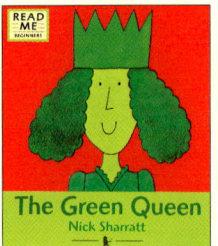
The Green Queen
Nick Sharratt

Read Me Story Plays are dramatized versions of favourite
stories, written for four or more voices to share.

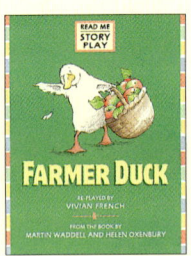
FARMER DUCK
RE-PLAYED BY
VIVIAN FRENCH
FROM THE BOOK BY
MARTIN WADDELL AND HELEN OXENBURY

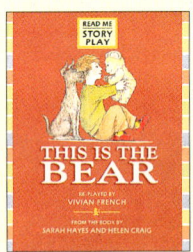
THIS IS THE BEAR
RE-PLAYED BY
VIVIAN FRENCH
FROM THE BOOK BY
SARAH HAYES AND HELEN CRAIG

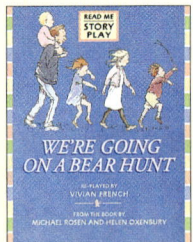
WE'RE GOING ON A BEAR HUNT
RE-PLAYED BY
VIVIAN FRENCH
FROM THE BOOK BY
MICHAEL ROSEN AND HELEN OXENBURY

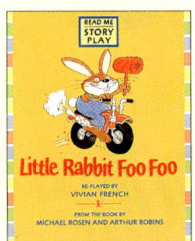
Little Rabbit Foo Foo
RE-PLAYED BY
VIVIAN FRENCH
FROM THE BOOK BY
MICHAEL ROSEN AND ARTHUR ROBINS

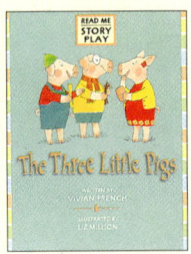
The Three Little Pigs
RE-TOLD BY
VIVIAN FRENCH
ILLUSTRATED BY
LIZ MILLION

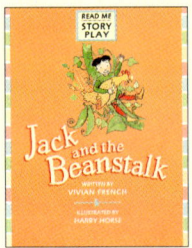
Jack and the Beanstalk
WRITTEN BY
VIVIAN FRENCH
ILLUSTRATED BY
HARRY HORSE

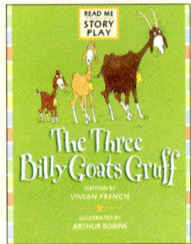
The Three Billy Goats Gruff
WRITTEN BY
VIVIAN FRENCH
ILLUSTRATED BY
ARTHUR ROBINS

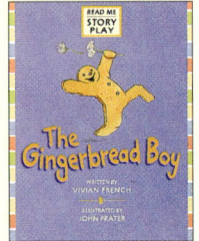
The Gingerbread Boy
WRITTEN BY
VIVIAN FRENCH
ILLUSTRATED BY
JOHN PRATER